BUSINE OWNER'S GUIDE TO AVOIDING MISTAKES

Common Errors Which Can Cost You Everything You Worked For

by Thomas Henry

Introduction – READ THIS FIRST

This book is NOT written by a Harvard MBA. This book is written by someone who has actually owned and managed businesses for 30 years. In other words, been there, done that.

There is no chit-chat or blah-blah-blah in this book. I am very direct and to the point and I don't waste my time or yours with bullsh*t. These chapters are short and succinct. If you allow yourself to be easily offended by my blunt manner or concepts you will deny yourself the opportunity to consider a different point of view.

I have read many books on developing your business, how to grow your business, how to succeed in business, how to start a business, how to finance a business --- and none of them tell you what NOT to do, and this is why I wrote this book.

Over the years I have had my disasters and successes, the lessons learned the hard way (why is it always like that?) and I learned what to do AFTER you screw something up or AFTER something screws you up (or AFTER someone screws you up!)

I felt that without having the knowledge of what NOT to do, you're only getting half the story, so I'm going to give you my best shot of the errors that I have seen and the mistakes which I have made, hopefully in order that you may avoid those same pitfalls yourself.

It has been written elsewhere that if you continue

to do the same things you've been doing, and believe you will somehow get different results than you have been getting --- you are legally insane and need to check yourself into the funny farm.

As I said, it's not just what you do right that helps you to succeed in business. It's avoiding those things that are pre-destined to turn out badly. I hope that this book is going to give you the ability to save yourself some pain and the derailing that will take your train off the track.

IN THIS BOOK I MAKE REFERENCE TO AND RECOMMENDATIONS FOR SEVERAL OTHER BOOKS WRITTEN BY OTHER AUTHORS. I ACCEPT NO COMPENSATION OF ANY KIND FOR RECOMMENDING OR FROM SALES OF THESE BOOKS. There are no links to any bookseller – if you want them, go find them yourself.

If you would like to have my best advice, write to me:

Thomas Henry
email@thomasadvice.club

SOMEONE IS GOING TO SAVE ME

I had a conversation with my son the other day and he told me about something which had happened recently in the town where he lives.

A convicted murderer broke out of prison and went looking for someplace to hide out. It was night and he happened to pick the house of a woman who lived alone. She heard her front door being kicked in and locked herself in her bedroom. On his way through the kitchen he picked up a knife and headed for the bedrooms.

Are you ready for this?

He found her locked bedroom and, knife in hand, kicked the door open. She had a loaded gun. She did not just buy the gun and stick it in a drawer with the naive attitude that this is what you do to protect yourself.

She took lessons in how to use the weapon. She learned how to clean it and care for it. She went to the range often and practiced shooting it.

When he came through her bedroom door she shot him between the eyes.

The police were interviewed about the incident and in the interview they said that every citizen needs to have the means to defend their home against an invasion such as this one. They made the point that the police cannot arrive before a crime is committed or even during a crime being committed. They will arrive after the crime is committed and the victim(s) is/are long dead. All the police are going to do is make a report.

Who is going to save you from employee/customer/hacking theft? Who is going to save you from being duped? Who is going to save you from any incident which has the potential of costing you your business? Who has your best interests at heart? Who is it that cares the most about whether you survive or go down the tubes?

That's right, bucky. It's you and only you. Avoid the delusion that when the sh*t hits the fan you will have someone there to bail you out. Think your lawyer is going to save you? He or she is going to pretend that they will to keep those fees flowing, but when you run out of bucks they'll be gone. Depending on someone else to have more concern about your business or financial well-being than you do is a pipe dream. Wake the fu*k up.

BEWARE OF THE BANKSTERS

I have heard many times business owners describe the "great working relationship" they have with their bank. Everything is all warm and fuzzy when they are letting the banksters suck off your profits with interest and fees. Banks lend out the money for high interest which you keep on deposit for little or no interest so the more you deposit for them to lend out the more they like you (at that time).

I am amazed at how many people pay bank fees for a checking account which probably earns no interest or keep so little eyesight on the account that it is often racking up astronomical fees for being overdrawn or return check charges. Banks love those customers. Banksters collect billions from them each year for their ineptitude. Don't play that game. Shop for a no fee account and never let the balance go near zero.

How about loans with "balloon payments" at the end? "Just refinance when that day comes" Really? How does that work out when your credit gets rejected because of some unforeseen change?

How about leasing vs buying? Leasing company official, "You will never own it. We do not ever sell to the customer at the end of the lease even if offered more than our usual buyers. We contract with our usual buyers to take 100% of our off lease items"

6

When you borrowed from the bank did you sign a personal guarantee regardless of the fact it was a corporation actually making the loan? Did you read that personal guarantee thoroughly before you signed it?

Was it a blanket guarantee which states that any loan from the bank now <u>or in the future</u> is covered by that blanket guarantee? So you are personally guaranteeing all loans made to the corporation or any other entity forever? What happens when you sell the business? Take in partners? Turn management over to others? Well, duhhhh.

You can be on the beach in Hawaii and get a call from your bank that they are taking money out of your personal account (or sending you a demand letter/filing a suit to collect etc. etc.) because a missed payment has accelerated the note and the entire sum is due and payable on demand. Which is today by 5 o'clock. Oh sh*t. Forgot about that blanket personal guarantee.

Where is that "great working relationship" now? Still feeling warm and fuzzy? Do you think those banksters won't throw you under the bus at the first opportunity to grab your assets? Do banking regulations prevent them from lying, stealing, and cheating? Check to see how many fines they have paid over the years for doing just that. Helping to disguise transactions from sanction countries. Laundering $883 million for drug dealers. Fraud, misrepresentation, it goes on and on. Seriously – do that – (Are you thinking, "Oh, but my bank is different. They value their customers.") Really? They put you first and not their own vested interest? Hmm. I

7

have a bridge to sell you!

Perhaps you think I am being way too cynical? Here is an easy way to test it – overdraw your account or skip a loan payment and stop by your bank to see that friendly smile once more. Oh? It isn't there? My oh my!

SOCIOPATHS AND PSYCHOPATHS

In the book "The Sociopath Next Door" by Harvard psychologist Martha Stout, a sociopath is described as a person who doesn't have guilt or remorse, or a sense of conscience. These devious, tricky people are approximately 4 percent of the U.S. population. One in twenty-five people you come in contact with on average. How many employees/acquaintances/friends/relatives do you have? Really? More than twenty-five?

Sociopaths are all not all serial killers or professional criminals, because in actual fact, they occupy high positions in corporations, they are government officials, and of course, executives in your bank. They have the ability to be absolutely charming when you first meet them. They have anecdotes, little stories to tell, and you are totally taken in by their charming sweet manners.

The DSM-IV criteria -- the gold standard for diagnosing mental disorders -- Dr. Stout says, lists seven characteristics: failure to conform to social norms, being deceitful and manipulating, being impulsive, being irritable or aggressive, being unconcerned about the safety of the self or anybody else, being consistently irresponsible, and being unconcerned and unremorseful for hurting or stealing. To be a sociopath, you need to have only three out of the seven of these symptoms.

Dr. Stout remarks that sociopaths have a curious charm about them, and a spontaneity that makes them interesting, saying that "someone who is unfettered by conscience can easily make us feel that our lives are tediously rule-bound and lackluster," and that joining them makes up for our dull existence.

I have had personal experience with these types and I can tell you that in the beginning you'll almost feel like you have found your soulmate and in the end of the relationship you are feeling as though you are dealing with the devil himself. They have no empathy and no conscience and they consider manipulation to be a normal activity. They can just suck you in to their agenda and when they're through with you, they will cast you aside like so much trash on the road.

Besides reading Dr. Stout's book, which should be mandatory, there is another book which will help you recognize and separate yourself from these characters: Snakes in Suits: When Psychopaths Go to Work by Dr. Paul Babiak and Dr. Robert D. Hare.

Revised and updated with the latest scientific research and case studies, the business classic offers a revealing look at psychopaths in the workplace—how to spot their destructive behavior and stop them from creating chaos.

All of us at some point have—or will—come into contact with psychopathic individuals. The danger they present may not be readily apparent because of their ability to charm, deceive, and manipulate. Although not necessarily criminal, their self-serving nature frequently is destructive to the organizations that employ them.

You need to be very aware when you come in contact with these people and at some point you will and they can and will cause you irreparable damage. These

10

two books give you the insight, information, and power to protect yourself and your company before it's too late.

Of course, if you happen to <u>be</u> a scumbag lowlife sociopath or psychopath these two books will help you learn ways to disguise who you really are (until it is too late for your victims!)

ANGER MANAGEMENT

A boss has a fight with the wife and at work takes it out on the employee. The employee feels badly treated by the boss and takes it out on co-workers and underlings. At the end of the day everyone gets into their cars and aggressively cut other drivers off in traffic. At home they have a fight with their spouse. And so it goes on.

When I came out of the service I was twenty years old and a very angry man. Two years of being in the jungle carrying a rifle everywhere, even to shower and sh*t, living with fear 24/7, never smiling or laughing. Pent up anger, ready to explode at whoever was close.

Frustration, hurt, annoyance, disappointment. It is all going to happen. To you. At the worst possible time in the worst possible way. But deciding the outcome is something which you can do in advance. Once emotions take over and your brain stops thinking is a little too late for rational thought.

Have a plan and avoid the regrets. You can piss off your best workers with your crappy attitude and then where are you? Are you subject to frequent outbursts? Do you "dress people down" with cutting remarks to destroy their self-esteem? Is your "constructive criticism" just thinly veiled sarcastic personal attacks? Is this any way to "build a team", "develop loyalty", or "earn respect"? Of course not.

12

What is it exactly that you are trying to accomplish? People are just trying to survive in this world, feed their families, educate their children. Just because they work for you doesn't make them unworthy of being treated with respect, does it?

I would like to give you my best shot on this. You may agree with me or disagree. Or maybe you will have a different opinion in the future. Doesn't matter – just have an open mind right now and see if you can grasp this concept.

All human emotions (not for the sociopaths or psychopaths) are based on only two root emotions, fear and love. Anger, envy, jealousy, judgment – all fear based. Fear of being made fun of, fear of someone hurting you or taking advantage of you, fear of someone else being richer/better looking/smarter than you. Fear of losing your love interest.

What you criticize/dislike in others is <u>exactly</u> what you see and don't like in <u>yourself</u>.

Here is an experiment I invite you to do. Become the observer. Listen carefully to everything that comes out of your mouth. Ask yourself this question: Is what I am saying based on fear or love?

I invite you to choose to live your life in love and not fear. Are you going to drive people away with your complaining and self-pity or are you going to be the magnet whom people gravitate to because of how you make them feel good about themselves? It is your choice.

Do you really want to "Make friends and influence people"? Being an asshole isn't going to do it for The love you receive is not what is important. It is only the love which you give that is important.

DON'T HIRE RELATIVES

Let's get one thing straight. Starting a business with your brother or cousin where you are equal partners from the get-go is not what I am talking about here. Although most partnerships seem to "shake hands and come out fighting" this is another subject entirely and not what this chapter is about.

One thing I have observed with small businesses is that as the business grows, the entrepreneur will look around and decide that this is his opportunity to help his siblings, cousins, brothers in law, or whatever fools they happen to be related to. They never think about what to do when it turns out that this relative occupying a position in their business is really incompetent, unqualified, can't do the job, and is costing a lot of money by being in this position? Maybe it is the job growing while they do not and it is time for new blood in the position. Maybe they are just losers leaching off a richer relative.

Now they ask themselves: "what am I going to do now? How am I going to fire my relative? How is that going to affect family life when we are all together?"

Do you think maybe firing that relative is going to maybe be something that will just continue to fester for years to come? Every time you have a family gathering someone that hates you because you cost them their job is going to be there. Or not show up because you will be there. Don't hire your relatives. Hire someone that gets the job based on their merit, not their family connection.

15

You're always going to make excuses and take crap from a family member that you would never do for a non-family member.

No matter how much you want to help your family, don't ever think that helping them by giving them a job in your business is a wise thing to do because it never is. Yes, it's true. Sometimes families go together and form a business and work together and it does succeed, but that's when they all come together to begin the business. If you are hiring your relative as an employee, then you are having to dictate to them as a manager to an employee. Do they ever take you as their boss or only as "Uncle Joe"? (Another topic is don't use your business for social engineering experiments. Hire only for competant ability and work ethic, not for any other reason regardless of how politically correct or currently fadish)

There was a reality show on TV for years of this family that owned a pawn shop in Chicago. Half the show consisted of the fights between the father and the son, the daughter and the father, the son and the daughter. Every day a new power struggle, every day some family member plotting behind the back of another family member. Hell on earth. Honestly, is this how you want to live your life?

"Oh, no, that would never happen to us. We love each other too much for that to happen."

Really, Bucky? Well, good luck with that!

16

PERSONAL LIFE VS. BUSINESS LIFE

Your personal life will interfere with, and affect in a negative or positive way, your business life. This is a fact.

Don't ever think it will not. You are not going to be an ethical business person and an unethical person in your personal life. You're not going be one kind of person in your business life and a totally different person in your personal life.

Remember these?
"What goes around comes around"
"As you sow, so shall you reap"
"The 12 laws of Karma"
"As you think, so are you"

You know every smartphone has a voice recorder, a video and a still camera built in? Do you know how many cameras connected to recording devices are in stores, houses, and streets & sidewalks? Nowadays, these cameras are literally everywhere.

Do you honestly have any idea how many times a day you are being recorded/videoed? People are always getting caught doing something stupid/dishonest/unethical when they least expect. Want to see yourself on the news for participating in something really embarrassing?

Here is an idea. Live your life like it is being videoed all the time. Everywhere. Those less-than-

17

honorable back office deals are avoidable and you will reap many times over the benefits of living an ethical life.

From Medium Magazine, "People are complicated. Faced with options, sometimes we choose according to the most short-sighted logic. Sometimes we try not to choose at all. We indulge in things that annoy us, degrade us, and even hurt us, and sometimes push away what might bring us relief. Other times, we don't mean to do this pushing, but our vices make it difficult to do anything eles. What to do, then; which way to go?"

You know all about how to be living a healthy lifestyle, keeping an active social life and maintaining a spiritual path, keeping your weight under control, getting your exercise, eating healthy food. This information is all available elsewhere and does not need to be repeated here.

Some of this I learned (the hard way) and if you listen you could save yourself a lot of grief.

It was a Saturday morning about 1:30 AM and I took my shower and put on my pajamas. I am in bed just going off to sleep. Suddenly I felt like someone had stepped on my chest. The pain was intense and I was short of breath. I told my wife that I thought I was having indigestion! She suggested that I go into the living room and sit down there until I felt better.

After awhile she asked if I felt any better and I told her it was getting worse. She asked if I wanted her to drive me to the ER and I told her I didn't think I could walk. She called 911 and four minutes later the EMT's were at my front door. Heart attack!

Five minutes after that the ambulance came and off I went into four hours of surgery and 6 months of returning to the hospital time after time for additional stents to be put in.

Why was that? Bad genes or plain bad luck? No way. It was cheeseburgers, french fies, chocolate malts, and no exercise. What is the difference between a billionaire confined to a hospital bed and the average guy confined to a hospital bed? You know the answer to that. Nothing. And isn't quality of life something you need to pay attention to?

My mantra was "My way or the highway" when I was in my twenties and running my first business. Arrogance is a disease of youth which hopefully gets mostly cured with age. If you treat people with respect, (and that means everyone) you can expect and deserve to be treated with respect also. Getting your way with fear and intimidation only works for a while. Ask Hitler and Mussilleni.

I remember a best man at a wedding who gave the toast to the couple as the best man does traditionally. And in that talk he said that the most important three words in a marriage were not "I love you."

He said the most important three words in a marriage were, "please, and thank you." Don't take your spouse for granted as if she has an obligation to wash

19

your dirty underwear, cook your food and clean your house. The only reason she does it is out of love for you.

There is no obligation on her part whatsoever to you and she's not your property. Taking your spouse for granted as if they were your servant because they're married to you is stupid thinking. Sooner or later she is going to get fed up with your crap and head for the exit. If you are not marrying someone you respect and that you will treat with respect for the rest of your life, don't get married.

Perhaps this is a good time to mention one more subject that can bite you in the ass when you least expect it. Here's the story:

A middle-age man has worked himself up to a management job and he is enjoying all the perks that come along with the job. One of those perks is his secretary which in newspeak is called "executive assistant." (Newspeak is why actresses are now called "actors", stewardesses are now called "flight attendants", Negroes are now called "African-Americans", and waitresses are now "servers". In the future perhaps all words used to criticize liberal social engineers will be banned from usage?)

Back to the story. Here is the guy, married for years, toiling away at his job, and he can't help but notice his assistant's beautiful legs in those short skirts. When she leans over his desk to flash him a bit of cleavage – well, you know the rest. Every guy finds himself thinking with the little head instead of the big head from time to time. He starts having an affair with that beautiful young girl and (wouldn't you know it?) before long the wife figures it out. Hey guys, wives always find out. Really doesn't take long. Every time. Without fail. You think you are going to get away with it and no one will ever be the wiser? Ha ha. Think again, Bucky.

Well, he's caught and he does everything to keep the little lady at home. Promises and swears to break it off immediately and never do it again. Ever. Tears in his eyes and begging on his knees.

She takes him back. Forgives and forgets. Well, never really forgets. Not really.

He gets rid of the pretty secretary (she always gets screwed in these situations in more than one way) and gets an old hag in her place. Everything is all peachy now and life goes on.

Until one Friday at 5:00 P.M. When he is about to leave and the boss rushes in with a stack of papers in his hand. Dumping these on our hero's desk he announces that these are for a client who is flying in the next morning and these need to be ready for him.

Our player picks up the phone and calls his wife, "Honey, the boss just dropped a ton of work on me and I have to work late tonight." She says OK and hangs up. Wait a minute – Isn't that exactly what he always said when he was having that affair with his secretary?

Every relationship, every single relationship,

depends on trust. Husband-wife, Boyfriend-girlfriend, siblings, partners, friendships. <u>Once trust is broken, the relationship is over.</u> Oh, yes, forgive and go on as before. No, it ain't going to happen. Suspicion has entered the picture and it isn't going away. The relationship as it used to be has ended. Don't believe it Bucky? Well, denial is not a river in Egypt.

Do you have true love? I have a scenario, if you will, that I ask married men. What it is really just a test of how much or how little they love their wife. You have heard the expression, "I love him/her more than life itself?" Really? Let's find out!

The two of you are trying out a new restaurant. You find it OK but have a difficult time locating a parking space close by. You finally wind ou leaving your car parked almost a block away on a rather dark street. You enjoy a great meal together, have a few strong beverages with lots of laughter and animated conversation, and you leave the restaurant.

You are walking back down that dimly lit street to your car when you are assaulted by a criminal with a gun who demands that you both empty your pockets and take off all your jewelry.

You see that his eyes are looking crazed and you realize this character is drugged up to the hilt and the hand holding the gun is shaking and it could go off at any moment. You are certain he does not intend to leave behind any witnesses.

So here's the question. You have three choices. Do you step in front of your wife and take the bullet? Do you step behind her? Or do you turn and run and call over your shoulder for her to run also?

If you actually love someone more than you love life itself, then stepping in front of her and giving her a chance to escape is the only option for you. If your answer is anything else, again – you probably should not be married.

And if you don't love someone more than life itself, you're married to the wrong person. It's as simple as that. If you treat your spouse with respect, never take her for granted, love her with all your heart and only look for ways to make her happy, you will be happy also. Happy wife, happy life, Bucky. You are who you are. What you do here you pay here and your personal life is your business life. You will not actually get away with anything because it will always get you in the end. One way or another. When you least expect.

Remember that, Bucky.

Never exchange what you want the most in life for what you want the most in the moment, because moments pass and life goes on ...

Author Unknown

PRIORITIZE OR HAVE A SEIZURE

Okay – you can read this one later. NO YOU CAN'T! GET YOUR ASS OVER HERE AND GET YOUR EYEBALLS ON THE PAGE!

This book is about avoiding problems in your business, and one of the biggest problems to overcome is the one where you delay or avoid the important tasks which need to be done now.

"If you choose to not deal with an issue, then you give up your right of control over the issue and it will select the path of least resistance."
— Susan Del Gatto

Thomas Henry Procrastination Excuse List (use these at your own risk)

"I'll do it tomorrow" means "I am going to forget about it until it becomes an emergency"

"Let me think about it and I'll give you an answer later" means "Let me forget about it and stop this pain of thinking"

"It doesn't matter" means "I'm afraid to do it or even think about it" or "It is too hard/time consuming"

"I just forgot to do it – (over and over)" means "I have a big-time resistance to doing this task"

"I can't take time to do it right now" means "I am really hoping the need to do this job is going to go away on its own."

"I have too much to do" means "I have no idea how to delegate or prioritize tasks so therefore I am swamped at all times"

"I just don't feel like doing it" means "I have no clue which tasks absolutely need to be done and which are pointless but if they are unpleasant they all are put into the same pot"

"Before I do that, I need to do this" means "I am putting off doing THAT for as long as I am putting off doing THIS" (Really? Isn't that special!)

"I need more information before I begin doing this task" means "When I study it to death for a thousand years maybe I'll think about getting around to doing it" Just so you know now, you will NEVER have enough information about ANYTHING, EVER. (And yet you need to gather all the info you can within the time allocated!)

Management putting off doing the important things which need to get done now is in the top five reasons businesses fail. If you are having a problem with that – get help. There are two books which I recommend: "Getting Things Done" by David Allen and "How to Make Sh*t Happen: Make more money, get in better shape, create epic relationships and control your life!" By Sean Whalen.

"I attribute my success to this: I never gave or took any excuse." Florance Nightengale.

Listen to this lady. Do not accept excuses and never make any yourself. It gets to be a habit and tough to break. You don't need it.

COMMON SENSE ISN'T COMMON

Elsewhere I mentioned the difference between street smart and book smart. Common sense is all about street smart, and so is surviving in a cut-throat business environment. There is so much "book smart" misinformation out there that sounds perfectly reasonable and logical but simply does not work in the real world.

Forgive me, but I'm going to digress here and I just have to do it. You are familiar with the Communist/socialist/liberal notion, "From each according to his ability, to each according to his needs." It sounds like a real sensible philosophy doesn't it? Our need for food, shelter, and clothing really is according to our bodily functions as a human being and does not change with our occupation, does it?

This is classic book smart. It doesn't work at all in the real world. Getting exactly the same compensation for doing well or doing poorly gives no motivation whatsoever. Want proof? Observe the average government worker. Making extra effort without getting extra reward doesn't work with humans or mammals.

In schools now the politically correct party line is to eliminate competition and give everyone a prize for being a participant. "Hurt feelings" by the losers of any competition are to be avoided at all costs. Personal courage and individual achievement are discouraged in favor of being a "team player." If you excel as an

27

individual student you are a nerd or a dweeb. Lack of "diversity" is given as a valid reason to eliminate advanced classes in math and other disciplines. Have you ever seen that bumper sticker that says, "My kid beat up your honor student"? Is dumbing everyone down to becoming a worker drone trapped into a lifetime of "easy monthly payments" the real goal of the "progressive" social elite?

Don't allow yourself to be pushed into snap decisions when there is no compelling reason to make a quick decision without additional information. All of us entrepreneurs have this tenancy to "fly by the seat of our pants" and this tends to get us in trouble more often than not. Every sales person worth their salt knows that closing the sale on the spot is dependent on creating urgency. The sale that is expiring, the countdown clock on web sites, and all the other tricks to force us into making a decision without having the facts we need to make an intelligent choice.

Under this category of Common Sense has to be the philosophy of "business is business, don't fall in love." For example: You have a location where you began. It has sentimental value. It reminds you of your humble beginnings. The employees who work there have been with you since the beginning. They went through the hard times with you. They waited sometimes to get paid, but they always stuck with you. They are like family. They know your kids. They give your family presents for their birthdays and Christmas.

The neighborhood has changed and your original

store is now a loser. Every month you have to put money in and it just goes down the rat hole. But you hang on to it thinking it will come back "some day". No it won't. Your loses will just continue to increase. It is sucking you dry. Bite the bullet. Take care of your people, but dump it or keep bleeding.

While we are on this subject, let's talk about the difference between a hobby and a business. You have gone through start-up and you are finding out that all the government permits or whatever are going to take longer than you think. Your suppliers who told you that you could have a thirty day account are now saying they need cash up front or cash on delivery. The carpenters/electricians/IT installers are all going past the time tables they told you they would do and they are all blaming the delays on each other. The signs/furniture/equipment you ordered well in advance is taking even longer to show up and your rent/payroll/utilities are going on without having the revenue to support them.

Realize all of these factors working together are going to eat up your capital and you have to be very careful spending only what you absolutely have to spend because you will always be spending more than you thought you would. Things are always going to have a bigger price tag than you planned for and so consequently, if you don't have the attitude of focusing on generating revenue, you actually do not have a business. You have a hobby. And the IRS defines a hobby as a business that doesn't make any money.

If you have a hobby, the IRS will not let you treat it as a business and they will not allow you to deduct your expenses. Because after all, this is your personal hobby. It's not a business because it doesn't make any money. The largest hobby in the world has to be Uber. Nine years from the date of founding and never made a dime to date!

When you're doing your planning, meaning that you actually have to create a business plan, your business plan has to have contingencies and contingencies are, as I've told you, things cost more than you expect, and revenue takes longer than you expect to come in and there are delays that are longer than you expect.

So all of these factors are going to require you to have capital backup and when you have that, then instead of having a catastrophe has closing your doors prematurely, you have the ability withstand those lean times until you're able to get the revenue coming in to adequately support the business and provide a profit.

Common sense. You just can't get along without it.

PARTNERSHIPS SMARTNERSHIPS

Partnerships are like marriages without the benefits. Some partners will disagree about every and any aspect of the business and breakups will happen. No matter how close friends/family/whatever they were in the past, being owners of a business can stress any relationship to the breaking point.

According to Noam Wasserman, a professor at the University of Southern California, within a year of starting their business 10% of co-founders will end their partnership. Within four years, 45% will break up. This means only slightly more than half of all partnerships will survive four years. (See how well that coordinates with the marital divorce rate?)

How to avoid trouble here? Have a contract containing an ironclad delay for vesting, regardless of how much cash and sweat equity a partner puts into the business. This could be for a year or it could be longer. The point here is that if someone wants to leave during that early period you are not going to be in court fighting or sucking precious capital out of the business to pay them off. No one has a partnership interest from day one – only after time has passed and then only for the remaining partners.

There needs to be a "constructive abandonment" provision that states what duties the partner is to perform and what hours they are to maintain to still be considered "on the job". After that there needs to be a defined

31

method of determining the value of the business and the departing partner's share. Paying them off quickly is the best remedy as dragging out any kind of fight can garner bad publicity and damage the business itself. Don't even think about going into a court fight unless you want an up close lesson into what blood sucking parasites attorneys can be.

Do 100% of partnerships turn out to be a bad idea in the end? Of course not, but you need to always have the "Plan B" available when what you are convinced could never happen, does.

This has been really short and to the point, but it may save you much grief and cash in the future. The point here is: Get it right going in and you won't get it in the end at the end.

SLACKING OFF

Ever have that feeling of "burned out"? Ever seen it in others? This is what can happen when you have too much on your plate and too little down time to recoup. Almost anyone who has started up a new business or taken on new responsibilities has found themselves working those 60 or 80 hour weeks with no end in sight.

What's the answer for this? In the case of a manager or business owner, it is acknowledging that others can do a detail you are doing and maybe even do it better. Outsource and delegate. My favorite book on this subject is "The 4-Hour Workweek: Escape 9-5, Live Anywhere, and Join the New Rich" by Timothy Ferriss. This is a business owner that was on the 80 hour a week grind stone and found a way to make a dramatic change to delegate and outsource which had a positive effect on his lifestyle.

It is easy to get into the "no one can do it better than me" mind set and fail to give responsibility (and accountability!) to others. Overloading yourself – and doing that to those you are working with – is only going to wear you out (and them) because no one can keep it up forever.

Which comes to the subject of this chapter, "Slacking Off". Perhaps you thought the previous advice was a pitch for slacking off and you are wondering if the title was advice. Nothing could be further from the truth.

Here's the scenario: You are beginning your work day by looking at the meetings you have scheduled (confirm them), the problems/complaints/disagreements you are expected to solve, and then you have the activities/tasks that you really enjoy doing and which give you a lot of personal satisfaction.

You know that you should handle the problems first and get them taken care of, but you are thinking, "They will still be there this afternoon, I will deal with them later." What do you call this? Procrastination? Poor management? Slacking off?

Remember the old question, "What do you want first, the good news or the bad news?" Rewarding yourself with those fun jobs after you take care of the not-so-fun stuff will give you more self esteem and less guilt for not being a weasel and ducking responsibility.

People tend to be mentally lazy and your subordinates/employees will be happy to turn over any "not-so-fun" item to you with the comment, "I don't know what to do about this."

Take each one of those one by one and ask yourself, "Have I given the person enough authority and training to handle this problem? Perhaps you can reduce your workload by taking steps to make your team more effective? Perhaps that "problem" is really an opportunity in disguise?

If you find the way to the 4 hour workweek like Timothy Ferriss or simply find yourself creating excuses

34

for not working the hours you have been working, the importance of prioritizing your work responsibilities is not diminished. The habit of separating tasks into three categories, "Has to be done now", "Has to be done eventually", and "Doesn't really matter if it ever gets done" keeps you focused and current. Without prioritizing work piles up and you become overwhelmed.

My favorite inventor and businessman was Thomas Edison. His quotes are thought provoking and motivational. Whenever you are getting burned out and feeling like making excuses for slacking off, read these again.

"I have not failed. I've just found 10,000 ways that won't work."

"Genius is one percent inspiration and ninety-nine percent perspiration."

"Many of life's failures are people who did not realize how close they were to success when they gave up."

This last one causes me to recall an oil man I met in Texas who would go to abandoned drilling sites where the previous drilling company had given up and pulled out some months or years earlier. He had a portable drill which he would use to drill as little as another ten to fifty feet and find oil. Keep in mind, drilling for oil is only done after an extensive geological survey is performed which shows the likelihood of finding an oil field. Drilling an abandoned site meant that the geological information already performed showed a high chance for oil to be discovered. The drill site was abandoned when the operator deemed it not worth spending more money in drilling. Did this gentleman find oil by drilling further down? Most of the time he did not. But enough times to make it worthwhile!

But these last two are my favorite quotes:
"Opportunity is missed by most people because it is dressed in overalls and looks like work."
"If we did all the things we are capable of, we would literally astound ourselves."

Do you meditate? Do you pray? Remember the book, "Think and Grow Rich"? Have you been aware of the scientific research into the notion that human thought alters reality? This may seem very "far out" to you but the science is valid and is being done according to strict protocols. What is interesting about this is that 5,000 year old records exist which state similar findings of today's researchers. A book on this subject by Lynne McTaggart is "The Intention Experiment" and it is excellent in my opinion. It turns out that,"Thoughts really are things." Who would know?

I am not trying to overload you here with concepts and notions that are well outside of your experience/studies. There is so much out there which is hard for us to get our minds around and yet holds so much promise for a better life experience. Please keep an open mind. Don't shut off what you don't understand or feel comfortable with. No one is trying to sell you any opinions or dogmas here – just the opposite – I just want you to allow yourself to learn and grow to the potential you have within you. Fair enough?

RUNNING OUT OF MONEY

You have probably seen how many times you will read this sage advice in publications about starting a business: "Have adequate capital." Sad to say, they never tell you exactly how much that is for any business or even what their definition of "adequate" is. To me that advice is as useful as telling someone to continue breathing for good health!

Supposedly the reason many new businesses go out of business is because of a shortage of capital, but that is a lie. I remember a new restaurant that opened and the interior decoration was absolutely gorgeous. Nothing had been spared to make this restaurant the most drop dead gorgeous looking place in the entire city.

On the first day of business, as is common practice in the industry, they invited all the restaurant workers from the surrounding restaurants to come and eat for free as they worked out the final bugs in preparation for the public grand opening the following day. Everyone oohed and awed over the lavish and expensive decorations.

When they opened their doors to the public, they only had enough money left to last for one week. It was not long enough for people to even find them. Even to know they existed. Even to go and try their food. After one week they closed the doors because they were completely out of money.

Was that a case of "not enough capital"? No it wasn't. It only had to do with how that capital was used. They had enough money to open their restaurant. But they chose to spend it on furnishings instead of operating capital.

A high tech California firm bought all new office furniture to the tune of $2,700 a chair so everyone would have an ergonomic, efficient, safe, and productive comfortable chair to sit in. Unfortunately, after they paid for all the installation of their computers and furniture and everything else, they had no money left. So consequently there was no money to pay employees and they closed the doors. Are you getting it? It's really not a case of not having adequate capital. It's really a case of how you use that capital.

If you expect that everything is going to cost more than you think, that all the government permits or whatever are going to take longer than you think, that you aren't going to get revenue coming in as soon as you think – then you will have budgeted in a contingency plan. All of these unexpected factors working together could eat up your capital very quickly unless you have a backup plan.

And so that means that you have to really be very careful, was spending only what you absolutely have to spend because you will always be spending more than you thought you would. Things are always going to have a bigger price tag than you planned for. You need to lever every supplier to the limit. Never pay cash for anything. Use a letter of credit only if you have to.

Do you need to buy your furniture and equipment new? Shop it to death and make low ball offers. Suppliers want money up front? Find another supplier who gives 30 days or at the least C.O.D. You're a new business, and they have a right to be concerned as to whether or not they will ever get paid, but business is business and if you don't lever every supplier, get every source of credit, find every way possible to do the job on the cheap, you could be one of those "he didn't have adequate capital" stories.

So when you're doing your planning and you have to do your planning, meaning that you actually have to create a business plan, your business plan has to have contingencies and contingencies are, as I've told you, things cost more than you expect, and revenue takes longer than you expect to come in and there are delays that are longer than you expect. So all of these factors are going to require you to have capital backup and when you have that, then instead of having a catastrophe closing your doors prematurely, you have the ability to make it through those lean times until you're able to get the revenue coming in to adequately support the business and provide a profit.

One thing that I have seen with small businesses is what I call the head in the sand activity. And that means simply that they ignore or don't want to see, don't want to look at, don't want to know about the negatives. They want to ignore the fact that inventories are mysteriously disappearing from their shelves or some other unknown activity is negatively impacting revenue.

Good controls, good inventory management, good bookkeeping practices will keep you from being a victim of those whose sticky fingers will do you in. Watch out for that bookkeeping employee who never takes a vacation.

DON'T BELIEVE IT!

What are the most deadly words in your business life? "Well, I assume that is correct."

Don't assume. Don't assume anything because mostly you're going to be wrong more often than you are going to be right. Famous saying, "To Assume is to make an Ass out of U and Me." Things look one way but in reality completely different – once you get into the details and find out the truth, anything may appear deceptively different on the surface from what it actually is.

"Assumptions are the termites of relationships."

You need to take the time to find out what the true story is and not just take it on the surface. What's an example of that? A good example of that would be your average newspaper. Every time I have been personally aware of the details of a story and then I've seen what is written in the newspaper. I've been amazed at how the story changes and how it gets misconstrued and even changed for political reasons.

In my town we have the Sentinel, which is known locally as the Slantinel. News articles are slanted according to whatever newspeak is in vogue, so the news isn't actually the news and amazingly they call it coverage and they call themselves journalists, but the fact of the matter is they're not journalists, they're propagandists and they march to the party line. Who calls the shots? The advertisers who supply the revenue for

41

the newspaper or network to exist? The government that regulates, taxes and licenses? The left leaning news team? Or all three? Or someone else we don't even know?

Psychology Today published the results of a study on lying and reported that the average number of lies told per day was 1.65 per person. The researchers felt that this number was too low and that many or most were lying about the extent of their lying! How many lies have you been told this week? This month? This year? How much fake news have you heard? Misrepresentations about everything and anything?

This next item seems to fit equally well in "Don't believe it" and "Common Sense" so I will put it here. And yes, it is one more "book smart" which is given as sage advice everywhere and is completely wrong in real life. This is the one where they tell you that before you do anything you need to form a corporation, LLC or whatever. You are told this will "shield" your personal assets from liability for anything you do in the name of the corporation or anything anyone does in your business.

Lawyers follow "the law of the deepest pocket" and add everyone individually into a lawsuit who is even remotely connected with the enterprise if they have any assets whatsoever. As an officer and a stockholder you will be included in any lawsuit with the claim that the corporation is your "alter ego" and "piercing the corporate veil" is easily accomplished. If you believe that forming a corporation will protect you from anything you are sadly mistaken. See what the I.R.S. does when you fail to send in your withholding taxes or what the state does when you hang onto those sales taxes a little too long?

President Ronald Reagan said, "Trust, but verify" and this expression was picked up by the TV series, "CSI." Actually, this is really good advice, isn't it? It can save you some grief and after all, this is what we are attempting to accomplish here, aren't we?

Question everything, Assume nothing, Learn the truth.

DON'T DIP YOUR PEN IN THE COMPANY INK

Would you agree with the notion that the biggest trouble you get into is the trouble you get <u>yourself</u> into? Why is it that men (oh yes, all of us) get ourselves into the biggest pickles when we think with the little head and not the big head?

This whole business of sexual harassment in the work place has been festering behind the scenes for as long as women first entered the job market. The sexually frustrated boss uses the position he wields over his female employees to coerce them into providing him with sexual favors to keep their jobs.

How creepy is that? A loser who women often find disgusting uses threats, veiled or otherwise, to get his jollies molesting women who may be desperately hanging on to their jobs in order to support their children. If you are of the mindset that this is OK as it "really is consensual, after all" I suggest you make an about-face and get your head on straight.

A man who "dates" his employees is really just a scumbag. What do you do when it seems that one of your female employees is coming on to you and you want to do something with her? Don't do it, bozo. Your workplace is not where personal relationships are to be fostered. You may be "in-between" a personal relationship at the time but this is the time you need to be strong and resist any temptations to date an employee.

What's that? Oh, one of your female employees is drop dead gorgeous and you have fallen in love with her? OK, that's great. Help her find a job elsewhere BEFORE you begin going out as a couple. That's right. Not after, not in the middle of. BEFORE bozo. Got it? Maybe she will find her new boss to be so much hotter than you are.

And if you are already married to someone else, FORGET IT. Men who cheat on their wives are just fundamentally dishonest. Didn't you vow to be faithful at your wedding? And what is your word worth? Sh*t? Because you lying to your "better half" means you are really lying to yourself, right bozo? Think about it.

OK – to recap this a bit: Keep your friggin' hands off your employees. Do it and you will be sorry. Treat everyone with respect and keep your distance. Hire and promote based on merit, not based on some "good old boys club" or favors you are getting off the clock. Keep your pecker in your pants, Bucky.

ADVERTISING SCAMVERTISING

At some point you may think it is a good idea to "create brand loyalty" or "increase traffic" etc. etc. and there are a zillion ad space salespeople, novelty items (750,000??) to put your name on, T-shirts, billboards and whatever. Are 10% of the business buyers for these products and services are benefiting from their purchase and maybe 90% are just wasting money that could have been used more effectively elsewhere? Is that pen or key chain really going to get you a new customer? Who are you giving it to? Your existing customer? What do you hope to gain from that?

When "pay per click" was invented you could at least tie your cost of advertising to the visitors to your web site. At least, you could until the advent of "click fraud" which saw over $5,000 disappear out of my account in one week with Google. The good news was that Google did inform me that I had indeed been a victim of click fraud and refunded me $32.00 of the $5,000 I lost. So you see, it all turned out well, just not for me.

Another time I bought an ad in a publication which was represented as a very good deal and to my target audience as well. When the publication was going to press I paid the balance owed and of course there was no printing but I did get to hear a really sad story about why it was never published. And the story included the reasons why my money could never be refunded.

Have you ever wondered about those "guaranteed

46

circulation numbers" you are given along with the rate card? Sometimes they have some very impressive "audit bureau" seal to gain your confidence. Have you ever driven around your neighborhood in the afternoon and seen all those morning papers just laying there unread? If that Sunday paper weighs five pounds then is anyone going to even find your ad? All publications have "promotional copies", over runs, returned copies, free subscriptions, etc. etc. so how many are actually reading that paper or magazine?

If you are just rolling the dice and hoping your ad will at least bring in enough new revenue to pay for it, don't do it. No, I am not saying all advertising is a rip-off, but I am saying that if you cannot measure the results of advertising in a particular medium accurately than you are best advised to use those funds elsewhere. Think about building a mailing list, loyalty programs for frequent customers, mailings and promotions to existing customers, reward programs for present customers referring a friend, etc. etc. At least do those first. Your present customers are your asset so use them wisely.

After all this, you may think I believe advertising is only a rat hole to pour money down. It doesn't have to be. And growing your business may well depend on when, where, how, and how much you advertise. So you are going to find ways to get your customers to tell you how they heard of you in the first place.

Your employees are going to get in the habit of inserting the question into the conversation and there will be an easy method you will find to collect and analyze this information. You are going to get your money's worth out of every nickel you spend to bring in a customer or client. Your future and the future of your business depends on just that.

FEELING GREEDY?

Did you ever see the movie with Robert Redford and Paul Newman called "The Sting"? Have you ever been enticed into doing something illegal/immoral/unethical for a big payoff at someone else' expense?

A business partner and I had founded a real estate investment company and our principal activity was buying single family houses and doing cosmetic improvements before putting them into a rent-to-own program. The additional money over the standard rental amount was to be applied to a down payment which they would be able to use eventually to convert the rental to a purchase. The benefit to us was that the additional amount was considered by the IRS to be a return of capital and therefore tax free. It was really a win-win situation for all involved.

I was in my office at the real estate investment company one morning. Two women came in and asked the receptionist for me by name. They had not called to set an appointment and I had never met them nor had any contact with them previously. I didn't know them from a hole in the ground. They told me they were court reporters and had a golden opportunity to make a lot of easy money.

I listened to their scheme as they laid it out and questioned them about the details but never found out any more about them personally. As they explained their

49

"golden opportunity" it came down to they had a victim which they intended to screw out of his money and assets. It wasn't just a little shady, they were planning an outright fraud on a specific individual.

One thought which came to mind was that I was to be the actual victim – that some lawyer had concocted this scheme and sent these two women to lure me into a trap – for what purpose I can only imagine. Whatever it was, I wasn't going to fall for the sting and so I bid them goodbye. Before they left, I asked them why they would want to commit some illegal act when it was possible to make all the money you wanted to make in the real estate business by helping people fulfill their dreams?

The two women did not answer my question, they just got up and left without saying a word.

Sooner or later someone is going to approach you with a surefire way to make a lot of easy money and nobody will ever find out about it. Yes they will! Any immoral/illegal/unethical act you commit or participate in will come back to haunt you in the future. It will be so tempting and if you are having cash flow problems and feeling desperate it may be very hard for you to have the backbone to say "no".

Remember the DeLorean Motor Company founded by John DeLorean? He was filmed appearing to accept money to take part in drug trafficking which was an elaborate government scheme to set him up. The video was released to the news media which delighted in playing those videos over and over on the nightly news.

50

His acquittal of all charges was ignored by the media because as good government lackeys big media sticks to the party line.

Ever heard the expression, "If you can't do the time, don't do the crime"? The law of Karma is going to catch you, baby. Sooner or later, when you least expect, that one little slip-up brings you down. Don't ever mess with the crap – or the crappy people – just look for ways to make people's lives better. And sleep like a baby. Honesty really is the best policy. Who would know?

"Happiness is when what you think, what you say, and what you do are in harmony."

Ghandi

KEEP YOUR PRESENCE

This book is about avoiding mistakes, but I also want to include some solutions to problems as well. The title of this chapter, Keep Your Presence, refers to the infrastructure a business needs to have from Day One (opening day) and yet you may not be ready to lease that floor in the bank building just yet.

The mistake to avoid here is to <u>not</u> have a physical street address, mailing address, phone number, fax number, internet web page and email address(es) setup before Day One.

No matter where you may be in the world, you can have all that in the U.S. for what amounts to be pocket change. So, if you happen to be in Sweden for example, and some one calls your U.S. number, you answer in Sweden. If someone sends a fax to your U.S. fax number, you receive it in Sweden. If someone mails a letter to your postal address in the U.S. Your mail can be opened at your instruction, scanned, and sent to you as a PDF. Your domain can be registered and hosted in the U.S. You can have a U.S. corporation without ever being in the U.S.

If you are in the U.S. You will still need all of the above so I will give you my best suggestions here. Once again, no referral fees of any kind are received by me from any of my recommendations in this book.

First, start with the postal address, and I will not

have a recommendation for this as mail services are located all over the country and you will have a preference for a specific state or city. Just know that the quality and range of services varies widely and you really do not want some sorry ass amateur handling your mail. How long in business? Is this just an add-on to their real business like a UPS store? Can they open and scan your mail? Will they post the names/return addresses of letters you receive? Will they dispose of junk mail? What other services are available?

Remember, the U.S. Post office has a form for you to fill out which is PS 1583 Application for Delivery of Mail Through Agent. Commercial **mail** receiving **agents** are required to have this form completed before providing service. The form kept available for inspection by the Postal Inspection Service and requires a valid residence or business address. This may seem like a catch-22 to you but with a little creativity you will be able to figure this out. Some international forwarding agents will give you a U.S. Address and help with the form regardless of where you may reside.

After you have your physical address you can use a post office box for your mailing address. I often see the local post office's physical address being used also with "unit #" instead of the box number. This can be a possible substitute for a physical address also, and now the Postal Service is offering this to box holders.

MagicJack sells a dongle to plug into a PC USB slot and then an ordinary phone can be plugged into the dongle. Even better, once you have your account established you can download an app for your smartphone and use it anywhere in the world there is WIFI service. You can choose area code for your phone number and with a decent WIFI signal it works well. You will need to use a US or Canadian address to buy it on the web site (www.magicjack.com) or pick one up at Best Buy. Magic Jack also offers a small business package. The small business service includes 3-way calling, call transfer, call waiting, caller ID, caller ID blocking, conference bridge, do not disturb, E911 service, enhanced call forwarding, extension dialing, mobile pp - ios & android, music on hold, online call logs, unlimited US and CA calling, and voicemail.

Google Voice offers you a single phone number to ring your home, work or mobile phones, a central voicemail inbox accessible over the Web and call screening capabilities. One of the core advantages of this service is that your Google Voice phone number can act as your master phone number - allowing you to program it on the fly to forward calls to whatever existing phone numbers you have and this can be very handy for sorting out the source of the call. Google Voice is a USA-only service. You cannot sign up for a Google Voice number from outside the USA, and a US-based forwarding phone number is needed to do so. Google voice numbers are free and can be forwarded to multiple numbers and the first one to pick up the call disconnects the others from the call. Instead of porting numbers each time you move you can simply change the numbers which you are forwarding to. The downside is that if you use a Google Voice number for your main business number you do not own the number, Google does.

PhoneTag is another option with voicemail to text functionality into your PBX or legacy voicemail platform, all received voice-mails are transcribed into text and sent to your mobile phone via SMS and/or email.

Several states offer online incorporation which means a company can be incorporated from anywhere. Nevada, New Mexico, and Wyoming have low fees and taxes and easy online service. Nevada can have a corporation act as the officer which gives a level of privacy.

Fax service is available which will give you a dedicated phone number from efax, hello fax, and others.

Executive suites are available world wide for meeting locations with office services. There is no reason for signing long term leases or otherwise pinning yourself down to facilities you will soon outgrow.

WASTING TIME

No matter who you are and no matter what you do, you have 24 hours in a day and 7 days in a week. Once it is gone, it is gone and never, ever coming back. Does it make sense to you to use some techniques to avoid losing valuable time? Yes? Read further:

Do you know someone who can take 30 minutes to give you 5 minutes of information? Some folks just love to hear themselves talk (I have had several tell me exactly that – they just love to hear the sound of their own voice.) Do not let them get away with it – tell them "I am in the middle of something here and you need to cut it short. Give it to me in one or two sentences"

I have read more than once the advice that no business call should last more than 5 minutes. There will be exceptions to the rule, but it is still a good rule. Don't be asking your callers about the wife and kids, stay on topic. No chit-chat.

You have heard of the 80/20 rule many times before, applied to different situations, but here is applies to customers/clients that waste your time far out of proportion to the bottom line profit they represent to you. 20% will amount to your biggest revenue producers and this is where you should spend 80% of your customer service time. The other 80% you spend 20% of your time with and if you have real time wasters who represent low revenue you will want to help them find someone else to do business with.

Your email/text messages/phone calls are a major interruption and time waster if you allow them to be. Do not let them take over your life. You are not an ER doctor (I believe) and if you get back to someone the next day the world will not come to an end. I read a sign in a print shop once that said, "I refuse to allow your lack of planning to become my emergency." Think about it.

Check your email once in mid-morning and once in mid-afternoon. Don't be reading all the crap and use another email for all those subscriptions or "enter your email to get this free blah blah blah."

Give yourself a day or two off a week from carrying a cell for business and never take it with you when you are going out to dinner or some social event. You should always have a cell with you for security reasons but you can get a prepaid cell phone service very cheap and use that one.

There are many time wasters you can identify and eliminate/reduce without much more than a rule change or a procedure change. Do not allow yourself to be used and abused by those who should be taking care of their own crap and not dumping it on you.

THE ONLY PROBLEM YOU WILL NEVER SOLVE

Yes, every problem does have a solution, even when we don't like the solution. (The solution to cancer is not chemotherapy – that only delays the inevitable, puts bucks into the pockets of the medical establishment, and buys false hope. The solution to cancer is death.) (No, not really!)

The only problem which has no solution is stupidity. Because it is an ongoing event, not a one-time event. I can give you a thousand examples of this but first let's identify why this is an important topic in a book of avoiding problems in your business. The reason is that stupid people can and will sink your ship. Before you go off thinking that this refers only to the stumble-bum class let me assure you that it does not. The most stupid people are sometimes very well educated – book smart not street smart – and they are going to cost you the biggest losses. One thing you have to realize is their twisted logic is always based on a "good reason" for doing something. Their inability to see the bigger picture and unintended consequences can be jaw dropping incredible.

Remember (or read about) when movie theater management would lock all the doors so no one could sneak in without paying and then hundreds of movie patrons would die in a fire as a result from being unable to get out through those locked doors? Still happens in night clubs occasionally.

Your only defense against having these termites working for you is to pay real close attention to the interview process where you ask lots of questions about decisions they made for other employers and why they did what they did. If you listen carefully (and do some investigating) you may be able to save yourself a lot of grief by keeping these disasters from working for you. You do want people who can make decisions and not run to you with every little insipid thing. What you don't want is the expense (oh yes, it will be very expensive) of underlings making constant and consistently stupid mistakes which are a result of "good intentions gone astray".

The other day I am in a store paying for my purchases with one of my international cards. These are MasterCard and Visa cards which are from banks located in other countries, worldwide. The clerk was tapping his fingers nervously on the table and then on the keyboard where he canceled the transaction after impatiently waiting a few seconds and then told me to reinsert the card. This fool couldn't give enough time for the transaction to go through – international cards take a little longer – he just kept canceling it over and over out of impatience and then announced the card "would not go through". I am sure that all of you have had similar experiences.

Just remember – someone actually hired this sh*thead. If you have one of these jerks slip by the hiring process and then you catch him – get rid of him immediately or suffer the consequences. They all have techniques to blame their stupidity on someone else or

59

something else and make it sound halfway plausible. Over their years of fu*king up they have become proficient at the blame game. Don't "give them the benefit of the doubt" – this asshole is lying to you and you need to call Luigi and Guido and have him swim with the fishes. Okay – that is a bit harsh but he still needs to go out the door ASAP.

To be fair, we have all made stupid mistakes from time to time – but this is not what I am referring to here. There is no consistent pattern to the occasional fu*kup. It's the pattern screw-up you need to separate yourself from, not those who learn from their infrequent errors in judgment. Politicians are experts at deflecting blame for their stupid mistakes. Listen to them say, "Mistakes were made." and never, "I made mistakes." The good old U.S.A. Is $22 trillion and change in debt? Sorry kids, we robbed you of your future.

"There is no cure for stupid."

Pamela Clare

Bio

I was in the military at the age of 17 and in southeast Asia for two tours back to back. I came out with anger issues, PTSD (still have it, don't touch me while I am sleeping), and thankfully all my fingers and toes.

Nothing to prepare me for a business career, would you say? But I went back to school (until I got bored with it) after I came out and then started my first company at the age of 24. From then on I founded, bought and sold businesses for the next 30 years. The consulting business I founded employed some of the most brilliant business minds in the country. Problem solving is what we did best and it is what I do now for select clients. There is just no substitute for cognitive thinking matched with the intuitive sense to see through to solving the real issues involved.

The major difference between book smart and street smart is the approach to the human element that always manages to throw a monkey wrench into whatever you may be trying to accomplish.

I enjoy finding solutions that work for difficult problems and I will talk to anyone from small, medium, or large business. I want you to know I am a very serious guy and I expect the same from you also. And I do look forward to talking to you and helping you. Contact me at the address below.

Thomas Henry
email@thomasadvice.club

Printed in Great Britain
by Amazon

23984703R00037